T0030982

THE
RUPTURE
TENSE

ALSO BY JENNY XIE

Eye Level

THE RUPTURE TENSE

POEMS

JENNY XIE

GRAYWOLF PRESS

This publication is made possible, in part, by the voters of Minnesota through a Minnesota State Arts Board Operating Support grant, thanks to a legislative appropriation from the arts and cultural heritage fund. Significant support has also been provided by the National Endowment for the Arts, the McKnight Foundation, the Lannan Foundation, the Amazon Literary Partnership, and other generous contributions from foundations, corporations, and individuals. To these organizations and individuals we offer our heartfelt thanks.

Published by Graywolf Press
212 Third Avenue North, Suite 485
Minneapolis, Minnesota 55401

www.graywolfpress.org

Published in the United States of America

ISBN 978-1-64445-201-1 (paperback)
ISBN 978-1-64445-185-4 (ebook)

2 4 6 8 9 7 5 3 1
First Graywolf Printing, 2022

Library of Congress Control Number: 2022930742

Cover design: Jeenee Lee

Cover art: Mirtha Dermisache. *Texto*, 1974-2011. Chromopalladium print on paper, 8 copies; 28 x 23 cm. Fajole, Florent & Daghero, Guillermo (Ed), Nîmes & París: Mangrove (Manglar), 2011. © Courtesy Legado Mirtha Dermisache, Buenos Aires, 2022.

Mirtha Dermisache's Estate protects the memory and production of the artist; continuous working in the diffusion of his biography and extensive *oeuvre*; collaborates with loans to institutions and in the curatorial and academic research. Contact: www.mirthadermisache.com / contacto@mirthadermisache.com

for my grandmothers

唐彥文
彭惠珍

continuing, all tenses

CONTENTS

PRESENT CONTINUOUS

THE
RUPTURE
TENSE

CONTROLLED EXPOSURE

No matter how artful the photographer, no matter how carefully posed his subject, the beholder feels an irresistible urge to search such a picture for the tiny spark of contingency, of the here and now, with which reality has (so to speak) seared the subject, to find the inconspicuous spot where in the immediacy of that long-forgotten moment the future nests so eloquently that we, looking back, may rediscover it.

—WALTER BENJAMIN

RED PUNCTA

By negative space, by forgetting's lining. By background: fabric where things seethe. Where fugitive looks and tung trees scrape open loose seams. In the far off, shame plants in earlobes and draws color. See how the background leaks out watery faces that haven't been rifled through. Such as the man in the crowd of thousands, running his tongue over the film scarring his teeth. Such as the woman, her fatty lids betraying her drowsing. The ones farther off, their heads angled away, mouthing the unrecoverable. The background is milky fog, is solitary, is sight that is untold. Edge closer. Friction from the future lies in the folds.

RED PUNCTA

Of the foreground, we will not speak. Look past the
blotted figures, stiff line that parts glaucous air from
ground's teeth. Forfeit faces. Alight instead on the
thin twine that screws hands together. Gelid
landscape, chromatics at life's edge, those pant
bottoms burnished to a peasant gray. Harbin in the
deepest of winter: eight stripped trees matching
eight individuals on their knees. Close the book,
they disappear. Open it, they're upright again.
A stone turned over: red. Beneath it, what we must
speak for. Growing lather sloughed off the dead.

MEMORY SOLDIER

In June 2020, the photographer Li Zhensheng died on a hospital bed in Queens, New York, of a cerebral hemorrhage, at the age of 79.

Torn color. That red of clots, flags, armbands. Of ropes of firecrackers that irradiate the past. Of eardrums, blasted doors to the mind. Of all that drains from opaque masses.

With the passage out of life, memory-images spill over an unarticulated margin, dragged across from the warm retinal currents of those who remain. And carried off is the purest of memory, anterior to image, which once swarmed like river water between the red banks of him.

Boyhood: He worships films with such fervor he pays for cinema tickets by collecting the aluminum of toothpaste sleeves. Brushing profligately, on occasion, to amass more tubes, to his grandmother's alarm.

Times when he couldn't afford a ticket, he stood outside the cinema just to listen to the sound of the film playing. There, his imagination grafted to the movement at the source of what he heard. When his friends emerged from the theater, he pressed the damp skin of their version against his own.

Years later, as a government-backed photojournalist, he made his own theater in cellulose nitrate.

For every propagandist photograph he published, he earned eight frames of film. The photographs that would never get approved, he slipped carefully into brown paper envelopes. Surplus hardening to archive.

The O of one mouth agape, of many eyes agape, of countless overlooked ruptures, deposited on the emerging print.

By the close of the Cultural Revolution, there were approximately 30,000 oilcloth-wrapped negatives hidden beneath his parquet floorboards.

The white-and-black sediment of Mao's *great disorder under heaven*.

Theater requires a domestication of spectators. But here, in Li's photographs, the spectators are simultaneously the actors, well-versed in plot points that click into place with a familiar rhythm, that align to the succinct script. The revolutionaries play their part in exposing the traitors, whose roles are inscribed crisply with heavy brush paint on placards. These actors are spectators of the other actors and spectators of themselves: a tight circuit.

Of the negatives published, one shows a provincial governor standing with his head hung, handfuls of freshly shorn hair piled softly on his right shoulder. Above hangs a portrait of Mao, whom the governor had the great misfortune of resembling too closely.

The terror of resembling power, of giving it another face, thereby diluting it. The governor is rebuked over 2,000 times, his head straining from the resemblance.

Does humiliation multiply, with a reverb, with every gaze that serves as a witness? The future lures with its many eyes, on which the fields of judgment may be ploughed and ploughed.

Thick character-posters drape around the necks of the scorned. Shame, as it accrues, pools and congeals behind the eyes; forming a barricade that forecloses a means of transport.

In another shot, the accused is captured from the rear left angle. His gray tunic, its hideously ripped padding, the cloth coming off in clots. It's unclear when he last washed. You can make out his closely cropped hair, the dry outline of cheekbones. His head angled to the ground. The camera's eye tamps down on thousands of faces before him, cracked open, pale watermelon seeds.

Li's camera can capture distance in a face. It can materialize a person's doubt, so transparent is his lens. Yet the distance between the seen and the known can't be crossed by the senses.

One photograph of monks, coerced into carrying a banner that reads, *To hell with Buddhist scriptures. They're dog shit.*

Shame's torment: those rolls and rolls of tedious, redundant speech.

On the same day, bodhisattva statues defaced and beheaded. Some donning elongated dunce caps, others melted down for metal.

The prints are black-and-white, which means the heavy stink of paint dousing the faces of those accused resembles blood or vice versa. Without color, one looks for other clues. The viscosity of the liquid. The evidence of cracks on the body, from which something velvet and opaque discharges.

There are others. The brutalized. The hanged. The stoned. The lashed. The suicides. The betrayed. The paranoid. The disappeared. The executed, slender backs to the firing squad. How close Li had to stand to acquire their expressions, close enough he could smell the spume of blood and of brain matter.

For months after, nausea dogged him. There are no photographs that evidence this.

Those were years of visual penury: in the folds of apartments and living spaces lay official family portraits, tucked away in manila envelopes and labelled incorrectly to disguise their contents. Father on the left, mother on the right, and the child, nestled in the middle. Straight postures. Not a wayward glance, a spontaneous gesture. But still, something to rustle through.

A lag of over forty years from when Li's photographs were taken and when the negatives were developed. When they emerge decades later, the living are abandoned by their logic and by what outpaces the frame.

Each time one of Li's photographs is viewed, the image is ingested and inwardly concealed. Coded into cells to cross-pollinate with other images in the mind. So follows the blurring, leaking, dissolving, reconstituting, flaring, scrambling, sharping, erasing.

Li Zhensheng, still hunting the realm of the unsayable with his camera lens, directing it toward the furnace of the living.

What darts in when the shutter opens, alongside the light that strikes clusters of silver halides? And what is it that recoils?

To watch a photograph. To reinscribe it with motion and the creases of time. The mouth binding to the bleared sun. The ferrous taste that arises from behind.

Can it be true? That every memory that solidifies into an image becomes a grave?

A photograph is no place to keep the dead.

They peer back at us from their positions and see, anchored in our eyes, a way out.

One can, therefore, read the future from these photographs, something hastening.

Place of nothing before.

Place of nothing after.

RED PUNCTA

Three boxy handbags seized from the governor's house, each crafted from synthetic leather, free from ornament and loud buckles. It is class betrayal made visible for all to see, a small exhibition for the townspeople. The only exposed faces in the photograph belong to the wristwatches, lined up carefully on cloth, as if recovered relics. The glare on glass conceals the watches' even pulse, plucked clean of hands. A man's character, stripped down to what he owns, yields to plain sight. Is easy to tame. Beneath the platform, the Red Guards' heads push ever so slightly against the frame.

RED PUNCTA

The revolutionary committee marches back from Harbin's rail station. A bleached Mao statue, no more than three feet tall, takes the lead. Cramped muscle. And two mangoes, encased in glass, each lifted by a soldier. The mangoes are a tribute to the originals: a gift to Mao from the Foreign Minister of Pakistan in August 1968. But too much labor for sweetness to yield, and so they're sent off to workers at Tsinghua University, who spend an evening holding and smelling them, passing each from hand to hand, careful not to let them bruise. One mango gets boiled whole, every worker is allowed a diluted spoonful. But here, in this photograph, the mangoes are made entirely of wax, rendering them immune to unevenness, those creases of the past tense. In the hive of the crowd, there are spectators who hold their breath.

RED PUNCTA

The girl's face gets caught in the shadow of a Mao placard, so in the print, she's the occluded presence. Around her, plump helium balloons and strings that tether them to fists. Right hands raised with copies of *The Little Red Book*. Nothing is as pronounced as the rash blood of youth, all power knows this. The other girls' bodies conduct a current of faith, but she stands outside of the circuit. Unknowability, a deep-reaching mold, rendering her all the more lucid. To be cleared of meaning, a kind of freedom only the opaque can claim. Even the loudest metaphor can't get a firm hold on her.

THE GAME

1. Forfeit the August you fell into an open manhole. Those years when people stole metal lids in the elasticity of nightfall and sold them off for grain money. Proceed forward fifty steps.

2. Abandon the two hours you spent tracing the chiseled characters on your mother's tombstone. How you drained your water bottle to loosen the inkpot. Chalky chrysanthemums you tore apart and tossed, so the vendor couldn't retrace your steps to reclaim them. Run a few hundred feet, loping through the gates of the burial ground.

3. Erase those years when the schools were shuttered across the nation. What else was there to do but chase your siblings on the factory floor where your parents shaved down wood planks? Where your mother lost a knuckle? You're ahead a dozen paces.

4. On the high-speed train from the eastern coast to the interior, the coarse skin of time sloughing off against the track. Worker, field, worker, field, field. Lighter, you're racing, slicing through thousands of miles.

5. What leaves with a person when they slide into a position vacated by the dead?

6. Oh, there's Mother. Asleep in the pigsty, breathing through the mouth. The thick edges of youth on her, upon which so much attaches. Go back two hundred meters.

7. Do you recall the year when the universities reopened? Taking the gaokao, the nerve-network of Chinese youth that summer. All that coiled energy, pressurized from those lost years, without a release valve. You're slowing down.

8. And what of those translations of Western classics, ferried over from their originals in English and French, and exchanged furtively among acquaintances? So battered they came to you rent of covers and whole chapters, openings and endings. Is that you, lagging behind?

9. To gain pace, shed superstition, shed customs, shed any spiritual feeling.

10. But tell me: What is spiritual feeling?

11. A shadow curdling behind concrete.

12. And how did your mother go? That stab of her solitude. The slackness, then the tightening of muscle tissue. Is she gone? Then unfasten each stitch of her from the margin.

13. If you can efface the query, smudge away the detail of what preceded her death, you'll slip effortlessly past this bend in time.

14. Are you not guilty? Does your silence not hold something pungent behind it? What's that steam running through your sentences?

15. To recall too much reveals you have an abundance to hide. To remember too little means you're surely lying. Retrieve the city along the river where the buildings' shadows have become strange. The one that houses a frugal green rail station, where someone you once knew exchanged bills for a one-way ticket.

16. There were faces from those years wilder than anything the eye could imagine on its own, some bright red.

17. You're stalled.

18. So you understand this is a game, yes? That the rules of the game allow for order, and order allows for perfection?

19. The future is charitable, makes countless offers. A sickle lopping paper, the spokes of questions. To refuse memory is modern, see?

20. The severance happens with a paring knife, slowly, then all at once.

21. What stays in you is a sanctioned secret. What ends in you ends.

22. In time, you'll grow into a silence so clean, it'll feel like being emptied.

23. Run ahead, run ahead.

NO VECTOR

In my city, time flows backward. . . . Within memory's labyrinth, one passage leads into another passage, one gate opens up to face another gate.

—BEI DAO, TRANS. JEFFREY YANG

Life is made up of separation.

—DAŠA DRNDIĆ

THE RUPTURE TENSE

The descent is occasion
     for an utterance.

Or perhaps the occasion for old scripts,
     those yielding wicks of false metaphors.

     Such as the linear zipper
     of return,
   which routes you
     past all burning.

Such as the guide who is no guide:
     only archetype, stale tropes.

No, here you'll find tiers upon tiers
   of checkpoints
     of your own making.

Forge papers, declare sovereignty.

     Blur the ratio that your body belongs
     more *here*

          than *there*
more *against* than *anywhere*.

A transpacific flight headed

into the crooked film reel of your origins.

Years staining from the inside out.

Wide shot:
Unmarked city lane, medium metropolis in China.
Damp concrete apartment blocks frame the view.

The night is hoarse—
we can hear it in the weather's amplifier.

    Itch of crickets' rhythm, shuffle of straw slippers.

      Search the alleyways with the ear
   and you'll catch voices from each unit's TV
           chattering past one another in currents.

When the eyes clamp, dreams appear in charred blue.

      Approaching, a hard node of feeling.

    And with it, memory-images cleaved from their echoes.

When the morning shivers through the windows,
  some damp spots, coins from another life, left on the pillow.

      Off camera, someone from long ago stages a return.

Cue expectation, a kind of frugality of the scene.

    There is movement and a spool of time
     and, therefore, we begin a narration.

        From the rupture, what is it that you see?

Departure hall, arrival hall.
                    Now the formal energy of a body appearing.

        Of the three decades that separate her
                    from the city of her birth, no metric of measure.

Clean lines of ramps and runways.
        Pressing digits onto glass for biometric tags.

    Here, buried on each pad of skin,
                the tight coil of one year joined to the tail of another.

Another shaving of her uploaded, in yet another database—
                    these high-fidelity traces.

        Mapping the borderlines
            of a codified arc,
        the usual patches of recognition
                            and resistance.

                            She empties:

mountain stream, white flowers

                stiffened by a few branches.

A misfire of allegiances

Shanghai is
Shanghai is

Shanghai

An iconography memorized from cinema.

Strips of pink and blue neon thrumming
on the jawline of capital.

Be it the eye that is screen, shivering.

Evening sprouts
electric umbilical cords.

Buildings chattering to one another
intoning cyclical obsessions.

Cutaway to rearview mirror of the airport taxi:

Cab driver, pointer finger in a pot of Tiger Balm,
dabbing on the temples and nasal septum for that sting of wakefulness

cutting through the edgeless fog of wage labor.

Staccato conversation to suss out her origins and class status.

The wide hinge of banalities.

Our nation's fragrant dream blares the propaganda poster
plastered, it seems, on every corner

over corrugated metal tines
and construction sites' flabs of skin.

梦::
a character you drag as a name,
twin trees obscuring evening's tide:
scabbed vision.

Dream: an illusion that doesn't open
by brute force, but by echo.

The underside of sleep
colored at someone else's expense.

No close-ups, no tight shots here.

Emotion rises to a stringent pitch
but refuses to spill.

Sound carries, location doesn't.

What doesn't get leached out, recedes.

And why not begin here

the sputter of this family:

Eastbound to the Shanghai Railway Station on a bullet train from Wuhu

Double shifts at the reception desk exchanged with a tight-lipped female coworker

The cousin insists on linking arms beneath the scholar trees, their stiff shadows crossing

I'm too thin, no matter what I eat, she announces, a grin fanning out into laughter

What is balanced between them is pruned syntax

Some beef ribbons tangled in chili broth, left untouched

Fifteen years since the last meal, when the middle cousin quelled cries in the toilet stall

All the streets here look the same to someone uncultured!

Trying to explain the uneasy impulse to run from where one was born

Just trees and lanes, trees and lanes, all the same. Is America like this?

Sometimes the deflection of questions is the hardest to take

Sister, she tosses out casually, so it's scraped of stiff edges

Is it leaving, rather than staying, that's unnatural?

To provoke the dry edge of a border, to tear a language out of one's life

Having never heard of what they call the "June Fourth Incident"

Pillows watered in the evening, again in the morning

Facts traded too often between hands become the nodules of questions

When she takes out her phone, a photo filter enlarges their pupils

Sister, would someone in America think of me as plain?

Symmetry in how neither of them matches the description

Someone like me will stay their whole life in one place. It's the natural order.

Paratactic and hang-dried of speech on the hotel bed

Faces warmed by the lanterns of screens

An intimacy built on unread gestures

So you're the lucky one, she murmurs, before leading the way into sleep

Money, all creased skin, sweating on what it touches.

Or money as pigment, red collapsing inward
        accruing on those lean black-and-white years.

A past rinsed clear of old tradition and filled in high-definition.

The youngest aunt, weeks before, asks over WeChat:

        What brings you back?
        Your cousin broke her smartphone.

                        She'll need another.

And this shame in detecting the mercenary in the maternal
                        —or is it the marginal?

As if there were a choice.
        As if shown two separate scenes, side by side,
                you, of all people, could make out the difference.

        As if you understand this:
experiencing one extremity
        amplifies the hunger for others,
                the luster of some cushioning.

        It's for you to let go of the gauzy thinking.

        Velocity of so many decades:
thin rubber against which
        you and her are ground.

Swift flashback: Tin bowl of braised river snails
at the edge of the shot, bottom right.

The family is loosened—one could say greasy
from happiness. We turn up the volume
on their asymmetric fortunes
clogged inside of them.

The needlehead pulls from the shell
all of the snail in one fluid motion.

For the young ones at the table, some wayward
sticky family lore
enters through the ears like flies.

That summer street-side fortune-tellers
reemerge from under bridges
offering the nerves of a future in place of dead tissue.

The eldest brother hands over ten kuai
to a seer who scans his face

and scams him gladly
by offering a few parsimonious phrases
jammed with sweetness.

The foretelling speaks to the kind
of life his daughter would wash into
down river, decades and decades from now.

You see, there isn't a price
            you can put on believing
fate can be extracted
            from the exhaustion of living.

To drain time
out of speed:
farmland beating

against the window
and then the spokes
of Nanjing.

Thin stream.

A pace that
inoculates
against
the past tense.

Then this fever
breaking
flesh tensed

huts vomited
over
the green.

The sentence hollowing
out to make
room for what

rubs against
two languages

verbs amassing
behind
the skin.

You lean
to make out
what's stuck

but at this rate
you can't
make out
anything.

To feel your trained Americanized senses separate out the oils of this country's

    :: Effluvium
    :: Fumes
    :: Penury
    :: Punctures
    :: Paradoxes
    :: Surveillance
    :: Extravagance
    :: Anonymities
    :: Dissolved longing
    :: Worker ethic
    :: Hiddenness
    :: Lamentation
    :: Nerves rendered numb

from the densities of those back where you came from

Trying to offer some true thing after the rustling. Going from one relative's apartment to another, drinking plain boiled water, taking a mouthful of overripe melon on a full stomach. Recycling the same phrases, wrung to drain the heat of multitudes. *Your health is good? Are you living well?*

Theater of gift giving, something like a relic of leaner times, when the only family member who had the luck to leave returned generously with sweets and cheap compact mirrors. The lure of foreignness, pressed lushly into cellophane wrappers. Now you purchase goods manufactured on this country's factory lines, shipped overseas to warehouses in your state, and return with them in wrapped boxes, tags attached to announce the mark of good numbers. The script of demurral, slow surprise. A pile of clearance Macy's colognes and tubes of Lancôme skin cream, Centrum Silver vitamins in economy-sized bottles, dyed leather wristlets with brand insignia, over which the family gathers, as if a hearth.

Afterward, peering at old albums from the 1960s featuring middle school classes, immutable faces multiplied, then sharpened into specificity. A thick brow, a jutting of the chin. Then a ripple of the person who sits next to you now, with her daily rationing of pills before her.

You don't look it.

You come from the same, you come from the distance.

She takes the knockoff Chanel sunglasses and adjusts her face

The high noon light here, lacerating

Better to hide this ugliness!

When her mouth opens, a row of teeth softened by an absence

My moon face—even rounder now from the medication

She sews the streets together with hurried steps

That familiar smell of damp concrete sinking into sewage

If I survive to next year, I'll have enough saved for an implant

Fermenting city blocks, fragrant with faces

Illnesses fed crudely into the translation tool, then Googled

I can't sleep, can you believe it? It's because you're finally here—

Indoors: a cheap mirror hung up for both utility and décor

A hot pink rose glued to the corner, and a wooden cross balanced on top

My intentions are good, I promise you, she cries into the phone

Money: profligate thief of dignity

Ashamed to serve you tea because *the leaves are too stale*

Spends half a day scouring for the best deal on a dinner package

To lose face, and she can't even stand her own

Sweet heaviness of watching her shave down numbers

With the fixed gaze of her new glass eye

I'm an old fool, reads the translated message in WeChat later that evening

Car horns gridding the city as you ride a taxi back to the riverside

We never even took a photo together

The youngest aunt, severed muscle

A question perforated, come undone

Against which you brush, and brush, and brush again

[Fog on the screen—
unwound forms against a hushed cage.]

During those years of blue ants, breast milk dried into dirt lines.
Wrest the baby away from the jeer of the nipple.
A milky halation: rice porridge over the fire.
Skim off the rice-clouded water for starch, add a pinch of salt for sodium.
The land torn open repeatedly is a famine.
The mouth torn open in staccato is an infant's
and so trickles in this attenuated broth.
The childhood torn open is the infant growing
into a pair of eyes that can see all
the ways the mind can go before the body.

Three nights a week at a senior center. Complimentary trips to the nearest market, a new pair of unbranded black sneakers. She saves them for regifting, though to whom, she hasn't assigned yet.

Nostologic, traced to the Greek for *a return home*, but with the echoes of aging, a second childhood.

The dimmest memories slide again into the station, diurnal. Slow shuffle of her late husband's dry feet, the automated cry of the village knife-sharpener shortly after sunrise. The neighbor who never paid back the five-yuan note, during those years when appetite outpaced ration coupons. And how her youngest cried for weeks for a crimson wool jacket, held together by wood buttons. *Just this once, Mama, not a ratty hand-me-down!*

Anger, if it ever held for long, sluiced to a trickle now.

Breaking off insults at the softest parts: the adjectives. She leaves them with nouns.

She holds on at an angle, so it never appeared that intimacy visited, sweat emerging on a stone.

If there's an afterlife, she's borrowing language from it.

One box of winter clothes left, with last year's scent still plump in them.

Not the return, but the bite of incoherence.

A kind of enlargement by withdrawal.
A kind of withdrawal by reentering.

Wuhu is unsentimental, easy with its gestures.

An enjambment of intimacies.

The rattle of four million on the drift of the Yangtze,
skin crusting around a water scar.

Such is the way of places and those
who are allowed no direction but forward,
no forward but *tear down*.

To keep the appetites strict.

To keep an ache particular, confused.

To keep linguistic acts misunderstood.

To keep the streets from unmaking
that which you filled yourself with
in alleys and between doorways

sticky-footed, skin-jaundiced

to tauten that blur of a world
you were just entering
as you left.

Q: *How does the clandestine behave?*

A: Sleeping tones.

A: Times when there's firmness beneath the surface, suggesting bloat.

A: Unclothing of names.

A: Decades when the negatives return in double exposure.

A: Grinding growth of debt.

A: Look at how risk elongates depending on the angle of exit.

See that bridge? We'd walk by those years and there'd be the accused rightists in paper dunce caps, heads down, and people throwing stones at them until they bled!

He murmurs, offhandedly, on the way to the bus depot.

Scabrous streets, dead nerves cushioned deep below.

There's barely a trace of old life in the city, though the cicadas speak with the same slant accent.

Then: *We packed you scallion crackers and buns. They charge too much up on the mountain.*

The passport his mind keeps, allowing him free entry between one year and the present.

No mention of the surgeries, the weight loss, the construction work he picks up from his daughter's boyfriend, who must refrain from drink, puff of white gauze over the IV puncture on his arm. Irony in how he keeps his pinky fingernails untrimmed, to broadcast his freedom from manual labor.

You learn to listen in at a lower register, the skimming talk between acquaintances, the recoil of a question.

Fight the urge to assemble lines out of this dailiness.

Collateral damage   is one way to put it
The pro-right hand   an anti-left land
Distance sickness   aids the forgetting
Murk of values and ideals   broadcast in two languages
Trained attachments   not to loosen our hold
Orient yourself   to the tit-for-tat

Forever abiding   in the untranslatable

They say	*There's no red thread to pull*
They say	*I'll tell you another time*
They say	*Your intention seals over your utterances*
They say	*Tell your words to play dead*
They say	*It's past so why peel back*
They say	*You don't match the description*
They say	*In these things you shouldn't stick the cord of your intellect*
They say	*It's only a cluster of sentences to untangle*
They say	*A little betrayal juts out from the truth*
They say	*You wouldn't understand with your own reflection in your eyes*
They say	*Talking and writing amounts to artifice*
They say	*You carry the smell of someone who wants too much*
They say	*Why must you keep these questions warm*
They say	*Even your dreamlife gives you away*
They say	*You're trying too hard to hammer it with thinking*
They say	*We speak facing away from you*
They say	*To make our language lighter*

And what did you understand of exile and closure?

It was the last season of easeful transfers, of the elective reentry.

Might as well prepare for the high contrast.

Might as well tune the nocturne, block out the lens.

And what did you understand about the occluding?

About VPNs, coded chats, the bitten and erratic ghosts?

About a kind of collective disfigurement that never goes corrected?

When you least expect it, feeling will congeal.

When you're from that far west, there's little to recover.

When your family sees you, they'll know you're foreign from the tides in the bloodstream.

When you tire of your own voice, break open the ears.

When the phone calls from overseas arrive, there'll be lipstick left on the heel of bread.

And when your youngest aunt gets shuttled to the ICU, trust me—

You'll be the last one to hear of it.

No part of myself had remained
      but no part had withdrawn   either

      Riding on the cramped backseat of her bike
  our heads bare   woozy from humidity

           We who are made   mostly of distance

         That pucker   of space   in the smallest of denominations

        Pedestrians   the wrestling   inside them
  some coming closer   to the surface

        A pang that doesn't shape itself
to be the same pang   as others

Two bodies   separated by a slab of air

     Slender answers   she gave you

        And she rode along in fluid strokes   steering—

                 never needing   to look back

            never searching   for alignment

And then the burst of wild sentiment

Their reflections announced in your water-logged eyes

Wiping off the diacritics of separation

in everything that leaves the wet edges of one's mouth

Seeing in them the gentlest of gestures

Ensconced in the most banal exchange: a heavier longing

Meaning, which cannot attach continuously

Language so remote, it dogs its scent back to infanthood

That it is all circular or close to it: the flare of the senses, the present hollowing

That to go back is to sever, to denarrate versions of the future

That memory is image, whole in itself

That we furnish the image internally

That the sonic dimension is asynchronous

That to make is to edit, and to edit is to scramble

That memory contains no vector

That we feel most deeply in the creases between utterances

That repetition in this life is an impossibility

That to shake open the mouth is to let something fall out of one's life

Out of one's life

Out of your own clotted ending-beginning

And why not start here:

DEEP STORAGE

He wrote me: I will have spent my life trying to understand the function of remembering, which is not the opposite of forgetting, but rather its lining.

—CHRIS MARKER

BROKEN PROVERBS

Catch a wrong accusation by its tense. Release it, and it'll chase after the smell of its owner.

In crowds, danger lies in the dormant fissures hidden in the ears.

Collective grief has no permanent address but countless vacant rooms.

Even the chaos of the revolution can't scrape nostalgia's residue off childhood.

It can take millennia to build an archive, seconds for it to turn into a gate.

When gifted a poultice, never let it expire or go to waste.

The safest form to assume is a mirror.

By the secret curdling inside, you preserve your health.

Shove a slogan down the throat enough times and it'll become an acquired taste.

A lie is a rhythm that marks truer things.

The suds of money, without fail, washes away the chorus.

Memory pulls the past out of its outlines and stuffs it back in all the wrong spaces.

Feel around for the lacerations inside the smeared laughter.

If a person lacks coherence, it's harder to measure the dignity you can extract from them.

In every still and quiet family, the past itches.

The dead do not end, they grow denser.

DEEP STORAGE

What remains [   ] of your [ ]other? The position of being [   ]? What
calendar [   ] were you [   ]? Did it [   ] marked, and [   ]
what surface? What raw texture was [   ] you slept, those
years before the triage of [   ]? Could you find [   ] the presence
of your [   ]? What dried on the racks by [   ]? Do you recall
the sounds that [   ] between crammed [   ]? At what year did
you stop [   ]? What [   ] cloth did you [   ]? How many
times a month [   ]? Can you illustrate [   ] of the first separation
without the use [   ]? Without [   ] violent gesture? What was
the first [   ] upon waking? What was the distance of [   ],
a footstep, a [   ]? What was [   ] being accused of? What did
your mother's throat [   ]? What did you insure your [   ]
against? What did [   ] mute? What monotonies did [   ]
time with? Who lived [   ]? What did you call [   ]? Can you name
[   ] were in the world? Whose [   ] bodies did you [   ]?
About what [   ] not speak? How thick [   ] grow? What
was the outer [   ]? Over [   ] did you and your siblings [   ]?
What rang [   ] a sister? In [   ] a [ ]other? What [   ]
water to the rim [   ]? When you were left [   ]? Did you
feel you ever [   ]? Whose [   ] did you [   ]? Whose
[   ] could you [   ], even when alone? Even [   ] alone?

"Wedding night [   ]
[   ] a pillow from [   ] neighbor."

"To [   ], even though
[   ] is disaster."

"[   ] blue."

"We [   ] in the middle [   ]
bit worms, [   ] plucked [   ] arms and [   ].
How else [   ] you stay [   ]?"

"[   ] centimeters."

1968 STEREOSCOPE

The daylight hours were for invented
inventories, the airplane posture of the body.
Collapse or cry out: that's guilt surely
snagging in the skin. To not think
what one thinks means one can
continue. Times she believes torment
is only an irregular rhythm hurrying her
toward whatever arrives in the next life.

When evening chews
through the sludge of daylight
that's permission to walk to the river.
The nephew keeps watch, still as a seed husk.
Something stirs and untenses in the banks.
It's her pulling threads of salt water
out of her own two eyes.

In the dark, your hands are hot
with your face: degrees of shame rising
now that there's no trotting out for struggle.
To make one's face move during the day
risks an aperture: squirming interior.
Only in the blue convulsions
of evening is your grief secure.

Have you ever seen a river turtle struggle
by another of its kind?
Seen a fish break its mind over a tear
in the fabric of its past?
To act in the present tense, thoughts few.
One wild creature has more freedom
than a hundred thousand of you.

1976 STEREOSCOPE

The sluice of teenage years lifts
with a murmur of green.
Huangshan pine in ink wash, a feel of lateness
and waiting's faint perimeter. Mao is dead,
waxy under electric lights and nitrogen gas.
It should be autumn, she should be a girl
still, but the years lodge thickly
and she doesn't know how to rupture
a decade out of this arid surface.

She lets her mind cool in the shadows,
absorbing radio announcements.
Rests a forehead against an arm
and turns toward sleep. No pull
of obligation, just a sliding.

The lid of a new decade coming down,
all those years asking yourself,
When will my real life begin?
Waiting on history for the gash of a red pen.
The schools will reopen, you think.
If there is joy from a man's death,
no one could say it, not even to one's family.
Your father's cheeks are dry archives.
Your face holds other faces and rests on your arm,
while informulable debts retract in the offing.

You don't feel the rim of your age, but.
After everything, you know better
than to expect life to yield
to soft explanation.

1977 STEREOSCOPE

The surprise is twofold:
the follow-through, and that it wasn't at all
uncommon. At least not in the heat of that decade
when background and class comprised the language
you didn't trust or understand
but had to speak constantly, under scrutiny.
The first time she reached for the severance,
it was soft white pills and her youngest found her
in the dark, and ran for aid several kilometers
headlong in the dark, without one wail
to rouse neighbors up on the hill.

Not then. One day, she'd leave her youngest
with a lesson on how to lie still
and exit the body all at once
to set on the remaining unmarked path.

All those years, the dead were just giving
you lessons on how to listen:
the way the present could erupt
when a circuitous answer to a question stalled
or how a memory at the surface could pinch
at a deeper one, until it inflamed
and bared its back.

What use was it trying to resist
the fading and trapping of
the mind's narrowing flame?

The left-behind and dead are alike: they travel
shouldering a simple bag, and form
the lightest of predictions
about how to make a passage.

EXPENDITURES

Soft, that tear of water. Which signals dreaming's low
boiling point. I draw down my eyelids, turn my head.

Here, the camera fuzzes. What remains out of focus
is the foreground, the waking forms.

Patterns arise in the sediment: when the eyes adjust
they're met with the stutter of faces seasoned.

In Anhui, my birth province:
my unconscious picks up the interference

of my relatives' dream language, of images that abide
in them. I am closest to their blood

when my memories dream
of theirs, and vice versa, *ad libitum*.

These relatives here can't afford self-pity.
If they've jotted down lines of verse, I'll never see them.

We carry some of the same nerves in the body,
but not a shared sense of how to exhaust history in ourselves.

Through time's stiffened membrane, mutual recognition presents complications.
Offerings of money and measurable affection, still the shared tongue.

And how can I be trustworthy with this mouth,
its tin roof of American English?

To aunts and cousins who speak at me with speed, I lend an ear.
I can't figure out the source, just the base sentiment.

I distance them at Wuhu train station, where their faces stay.
Days later, I find sutures of words dampening against the page.

POSTMEMORY

We take on the names of the deceased, give them new voices. —Celina Su

Struggles we had
a name for and those
for which we didn't.

Some matted
from one
generation
to the next.

Occasionally we
were released
from one
struggle though
we didn't
detect it.

—

Everything carried
vertically
from north
to south
south becoming
north
and down.

The past moves like this—

The body, too, like this—

–

All the bodies
we take
on over
lifetimes
descending
into harder
rock

bitten fingers
stranger aches.

–

Growing is forgetting
and creation is
discreation
with a new head
at the fore

where the most
aggressive eyes
grow.

—

All this gaining
and letting go
honed along
the sharpest edges
of this life's perimeter.

—

Surely
someone standing
to make a profit.

—

Nature reuses
plotlines
not wanting
to waste
a thing.

And so we get sewn
back into
our origins.

The deeper
textures.

REACHING SATURATION

All new images leave your thinking askew.

And wouldn't you know—you wouldn't
recognize these streets even if they translated you
phoneme by phoneme.

If feeling comes, some form of modern distance will clot it.

In your alogical ways, you make a foolish bargain:
you ask to be a native again—naive
as you are, with steadfast eyes.

Some knavery in desire, some echo.

What more is there to say about the way
your homeland's forehead degrades?

All stitching of narrative alienates.

Murky grows the sky in Brooklyn, upward from the night's stiff stem.

But not so in Hefei!

In Hefei, darkness
emerges in rough spots

chafed from the back of street noise.

Dusk's wide mouth
muffles the city statues

This parsimony of detail
so the still image will last

Incursion of the city's lymph
pushing against your tissues

Crust cut off economically
from the harbor

Each life, rustling the folds of the year

Time: scented differently here

Some futures take root.

Bulldozers masticating between two city blocks

where the lining of a luxury high-rise thickens.

Aphasia runs through you.

Lapping at the sight of other people:

the mind feeds on synonyms, approximations.

Gray slosh of the Huangpu against chrome and metal splinter.

Stitches in the phosphorescing air.

But the old city slides out of one alley. Not just from the architecture, but the way of speaking, one syllable under another. The touching of speech, the air ionized, some keys left at the doorway where a mourning dove offers seasoned murmurs. From pairs of wet eyes, and from street names, which bear the mark of a past ground under.

Slip out and the anesthesia rubs down the nostrils.

Flavors of knowing coming off bodies moving irrationally on the city grid.

Run a cleaning agent
   through your utterances.

Doubtless this makes
the lacunae
   effervescent.

   Obscure the republic
of memory
    behind you
to ensure everything stays
     encoded in the future.

But who was it that said so?

It's when the signal
   is weak that you begin
  to develop
    a need
   for an antenna.

Silences reaching saturation

No one can read the dead
in their creasings

Not even an afterlife
of nostalgia to inherit

Here comes the vapor of faces
and a skyline widened by speculum

It isn't the surface tension
in conversations

What is encoded in red lines
is a collective debt paid

Wrested from the place
where the fog's tongue smashes the mountainside.

Muddy mind churning with muddy thinking.

Foreheads sliding against windowpanes.

Silence has the largest ear, wrote Lan Lan.

Anaphora in how each day emerges
with such subtle trembling.

Kin who wrote in strophes on fields
and marked years by
the yield, only later
to let the seasons erase them.

If the ancestors can see, only they see
which of us are gates and which
of us are partitions.

Shop owners and migrant workers
bet against your boredom with theirs.

These swift looks go down easy.

The untranslatability of
the tapestry of wage workers, migrants—
like the uncle who keeps his pinky nail long
to dig himself out of his own class position.

If there's dissonance in the air
it's between dreamlife and waking:

One is kept cracked.
The other, darkly greased.

RMB 50 to enter through the temple doors.

RMB 5 for a bundle of incense sticks to make a prayer ascend,
under the yellow construction crane's one gimlet eye.

Whatever cost for the other realm to eat the prayer,
curled like a rose:
a limit we're kept from knowing.

Bend the vertebrae in the four directions.

The black Audis hide ears,
they pull up alongside with special passes.

And monks deepen the colors of their soft garments,
their fingers pecking at Samsung phones.

Watching from varying heights, those bodhisattvas.
Their mute reach:
tapered hands, mouths refusing to lengthen.

A figure making its way to the temple   3:42 a.m.
bone in the wind's   throat

The tongue cleans   the bowl
The forehead soaks up   the wooden floor

Shave off the metaphor   until it's lean
until it's purposeless

Sediment of the day   wiped clean
Sitting still   pulling at the root   of consciousness

Then comes the needlepoint   of language
which makes a thought   visible

Construction cranes
        stir a building's shadow
   to keep it from cooling.

Forty or so years ago, this view was just farmland
        but now bony angles protrude from fog

   all those straight lines
      scrambling for historical substance.

What does it mean to answer by a name
    in this city blur?

                To recede so deeply into a verb
              that one simply dissolves.

How even the names on these gravestones
tear into new forms
    as the local weather works
  its way into them.

City streets' coughing is a scattering of coins.

The lozenge, lunar.

Think of the years of living two lives,
          two kinds of speech, two kinds of silences.
     Mendacity a kind of daily ritual.

     Eavesdropping on neighbors.
          Turning each utterance to its backside
     to peer at where it was made.

     Every face hides a stone and beside it a lamp.

The hush is at a pitch that one can
          only make it out collectively.

[secret language spoken]

Bodies that jostle, press, heave.

The physicality of these streets.

And money that leaks, warmth

in the city's erogenous zones.

Those who get ahead

adopt the metal crane's posture,

grow in the direction of the skyline.

We keep the turbulence inward

unlike in days past.

Who knows what

will reawaken it

from its slumber?

The younger generations keep few secrets.

A secret smacks of privations.

Privatization of nonspeech,
            overexposures of phrases.

We're learning, too.

The rate at which silence appreciates
                    when neglected.

                Letting go is cheap.

        Forgetting, the cheapest.

PRESENT CONTINUOUS

we deal with a permanent voyage,
the becoming of that which itself had
become

—ETEL ADNAN

There is no answer, there is no echo
Just the torches of ghosts, illuminating my whole life...

—DUO DUO, TRANS. GREGORY LEE

MEETING PLACES

The world clangs!
    Death barks back in the furred dark.

     In the recesses of newsprint
         you trace the ragged line
      where one country joins
         with another by torturous stitches

        and feel convulsions
     along your midpoint.

The world stops clanging.

     Death licks at its privates.

          And then you turn the page.

Pessoa, two weeks before his end:
      I am merely the place
      Where things are thought or felt.

The land has ways
      of lancing and draining the eternal.

      Undifferentiated language that advances and recedes.

          Binding dissolutions.

Currents of violence carried in the organs,
    the corners of the mouth
      and through one's grammar.

    Mountains bearing the same patterning.
Vascular from an aerial view.

      And why must it all return to the body?

    A cloud shadow keeps a slag
of the hillside in relief
      while simultaneously
    time congeals, from the edges first.

The rush of forms in all directions.

    And stillness yielding.
      In the eyes of the city center.

MISCONJUGATE

When the distance between subject and verb is longer
than a tongue's measurement
I strike myself with the belt of a wrong tense.

Where it hits, a band of skin blanches, white like a hen.

No surprise that I'm more verb than subject.

No surprise that time, like an automobile, bleeds
down the congealed mountainsides of me.

With age, it's harder to make out good deeds,
which rinse clear after several lathers.

All I know is when I'm virtuous, I dare not disturb
the wires of the underworld.

My present tenses are just basins
where endings approach room temperature.

THE MADE WORLD

Your ear moves along one swarm of conversation
to another, then alights on a dog's stiff bark
in a cubed cornflower house up the hill.

How hard the city center has worked for this,
how easily the churches gather, with their brushed ribs.

Some words tossed off like beads, some pepper
cooling on the lip of a bowl.

Small glances, from afar, that one keeps in the front pockets.

Blurry forms are stored elsewhere, in the camera,
stacked along streets of ochre and rose.

Attention's formidable property. You spend it quickly.

Crumbling rock with your feet
along alleyways, those loose couplets.
You mistake this openness for waking

but it's a trick of the landscape.
We, who are made and unmade
by the dark mass of the unseen.

This far inland, emptying out feels both distant and near.

TERRITORIES UNMAPPED

Rehearsal of childhood after childhood has passed

A manner of lucidity when the mind lies in the same direction as the body

Sensation of sleep mixing in with sight as a thickening agent

Surfaces that prove harder to plumb than depths

A realization built entirely on being protected from harder truths

The stiff seam between a return and a repetition

Reading the silence after a question backward

Gap between understanding pain and someone else's cries

The guesswork we make of the remainder of our lives

PRESENT CONTINUOUS

In the sweetness of the mountain pass, the severity of lines.

Thick saguaros, stabs of gold to the east and west of me.
Even so, nerves quelled by a dry wind.

Truth is, I'm just two brushstrokes—no more, no lesser.

Even without a center, I can sense forces urging
my life back inside invisible coordinates.

The root of forgetting is the constant
rebuilding of the interior.
Is an exhausted sun licking the land clean.

Forgive me—

I grow sleepless in August.
Answering to a whistle even I can't hear.

Tell me again about the arrogance of the restless.

When is it enough—staying still?
Absorbing the echoing of tenses?

UNIT OF MEASURE

Time so undifferentiated
it's symmetry without a face.
Without circumference
and leapt clean from outline.

Here: lid of each day.
Cream of fool's filling.

Jump cut after jump cut
and none of the cadence
of suture.

Measure by measure
those robed in temples
bring the breath to the body's surface:
their sit-bones molded to buckwheat cushions
their spines upright as if held
in suspension by fishing rods.

On Kawara, who mixed fresh
his reds, blacks, and blues
on each day's rim
then set time in its casing
with the slim sewing of pencil and then brush.

Did he see how weeks soften and lose shape
with a ribbon of white fat at the edges?

How sleep gathers within the eyes,
an infection that heals each evening?

Oh, motion sickness of the minute hand
that came centuries after the hour,
trimming the day down to property and to size.

To fill time or to decant it?

That which must be ingested undiluted.

Which passes from my body to yours.

IN SEARCH OF

It wasn't   the knob of sun

Or grainy currents   crossing the eye

that invites thought   that you've finally arrived

at the clearest understanding   this very instant on the Huangpu River

where the mind is serrated   dragging its way

All this thinking   thousands upon thousands along the river and inland

and still meaning is heavier   than the bodies we yoke it to

Surely for this reason   death must   announce itself

again and again   in such sour language

so we may live closer   to the senses   the sweat of the unsayable

Moments when we feel history   pulling from behind

the eyes   the mouth   hooked

But the remainder   of this life

is still millions of kilometers away   from being born

DISTANCE SICKNESS

In memory of 唐彦文 *(1932–1977)*

Where to locate you in the interminable station?

Nowhere goes clean through the static of decades without hitting a nerve

Nowhere are you coterminous with the right coordinates, the red time stamp

Nowhere does the skin unbind along the longitude of the page

Steam of a childhood episode erodes your sense of sound

Grandmother bearing the infant on the hip, using the communal wash closet

Entire decade where the verb *to want* arrived posthumously

To relive is the snarl of description, worked over repeatedly in the mind

The girl vomits up pilfered blue gumballs and thin sugar paste

New hues wash into the scene, pop songs written in the first person

Unable to sharpen her eyes, she loses most sense of proportion and scale

The child commits to language and things calcify in separation

Nowhere does the color of your skin awaken into current

The city infected quickly, rash of glass and steel

Workers cropping up by the factory towns, waiting to be plucked

Hairs of every head in the family stirred by the tendons of the wind

A verb and its likeness collude to make time full of repetitions

One exam result becomes a way station, and then another

The rising appetite of youth rinses off in red

Heart failure and macular degeneration and something diagnosis can't hang language on

Nowhere am I rubbing a filament of 1958 against 2020

Nowhere is there a visual shock, two years sparking an omitted detail

Somewhere a generation of faces melts onto the last generation's

Somewhere we keep attaching to the boundless unknowable

Nowhere are you filling in the fovea of our eyes with calligraphy ink

Nowhere does the memory-image not quiver

Somewhere the shadow of your language catches on my ear

Somewhere the mouth spills with the solutes of memory, which thicken into something altogether different

Without provocation, the subject dies twice. The first time, in the murk of benign guessing: illness, poor health, medicinal odors, an organ refusing the heed of a metronome. The second, by her own hand, her eldest daughter jams this fact into a sentence, and from there, an interminable release.

And so: distance is introduced, a bulb of epinephrine. Shifts in the air pressure. A new verb eats through the pith of what-came-before. Fugitive. Beyond all limits, where you reside.

:: Not the face, but translucent gray spots, as if the face has been drained through

:: Not the adhesion of hardship, but what gets seamed into desire

:: Not the closing down of an expression, but the fluidity of cloaked forms

:: Not the bitten edge of the border, but what walks through

:: Not the marks of language, but a springing into

ALTERNATE ENDINGS:

You are milky and restless: a nocturne caught. *Hush*. Tucked inside the padding of mouth, against which coiled language gets absorbed. Your questions start to thin, webbing at the edges. Soon after, the present tense short-circuits. Because my own mouth is open when I look toward your direction, your face is smeared on all my vowels. When I cry out, pieces of you are carried off in quick, sharp drifts.

Closing your eyes, you point a camera at us. After which we blur and multiply, blur and remain fixed. Refugees in the nation of the seen. If you can't see us, we can't see you.

A person lost becomes a hook lowered into the depths of an echo. *Are you there?* we call out. *Are you there? Are you there? Are you there?*

In the beginning there were knots. A deeper emptying, some passage grammar can't fit through.

I write line and line and line. Stitch you into a pronoun.

Tell me, what is a poem to you?

Anything that continues.

Anything can contain you.

Your coarse black hair plaited tight down two sides

The visual input shores up a density

What I took you for: pressed between sheets of plastic   prosody of black and white

A firing of electrical pulses across

No bigger than two thumbs   one stacked atop the other

Your silence strains   *against what*

All year I wear you on my face   to move backward

Farther from death than I am   fathomless

The afterlife collects sentences of varying lengths.

Endings suppurating, beginnings crusting over.

Time, you see now, is an inheritance that marks everyone as a spendthrift—
how painful.

Small mouth: the unknowable answers neither slow nor quick.

To mix sleep with some language slurry.

To see the head polishing the pillow with so many questions.

Thoughts casting a dye.

As you age, childhood's gradient intensifies.

When spring comes around, you carry the weight of spring.

When summer comes around, you carry the weight of summer.

When fall comes around, you carry the weight of fall.

When winter comes around, your pages fall open.

And you, all future tense, leak through.

NOTES

RED PUNCTA

These poems were generated in response to black-and-white photographs shot by Li Zhensheng during the Chinese Cultural Revolution. Over the years of the Revolution (1966–1976), Li took close to 100,000 photographs, in what comprises one of the most nuanced and comprehensive visual records of the decade.

MEMORY SOLDIER

"Memory Soldier" and the "Red Puncta" poems owe a large debt to *Red-Color News Soldier* (Robert Pledge, ed., Phaidon Press), which served as the primary source of information about Li Zhensheng's life and his trajectory as a staff photographer for the state-owned *Heilongjiang Daily*.

THE GAME

Rule 18 derives inspiration from a line of Don DeLillo's, excerpted from an interview conducted in *Contemporary Literature*: "Games provide a frame in which we can try to be perfect."

THE RUPTURE TENSE

This poem is dedicated to my family in Anhui, China.

DEEP STORAGE

This poem is drawn from conversations with my paternal grandmother, 彭惠珍, and dedicated to her.

1968 STEREOSCOPE, 1976 STEREOSCOPE, and 1977 STEREOSCOPE

This sequence is drawn from accounts of relatives who lived through the Chinese Cultural Revolution. The form plays with the mechanism of the stereoscope, a viewing device that creates depth of vision through the juxtaposition of two separate images.

POSTMEMORY

The title refers to Marianne Hirsch's concept of "postmemory," which Hirsch defines as the "relationship that the 'generation after' bears to the personal, collective, and cultural trauma of those who came before—to experiences they 'remember' only by means of the stories, images, and behaviors among which they grew up."

REACHING SATURATION

Margaret Hillenbrand's *Negative Exposures: Knowing What Not to Know in Contemporary China* (Duke University Press) enriched this poem considerably through its arguments and analyses.

THE MADE WORLD

"This far inland" is a phrase borrowed from C. S. Giscombe's *Prairie Style* (Dalkey Archive Press).

DISTANCE SICKNESS

The title of the poem is a phrase from Hisham Matar's *The Return: Fathers, Sons and the Land in Between* (Random House).

ACKNOWLEDGMENTS

Grateful acknowledgment is given to the editors and staff of the following publications where versions of several of these poems initially appeared: *Ambit, Conjunctions, Jewish Currents, The Kenyon Review, The Nation, Ploughshares, Poetry London, The Poetry Review, A Public Space, The Rumpus, The Yale Review*.

Thank you to composer Anthony Cheung for weaving several poems from this collection into *the echoing of tenses*, a song cycle commissioned for the American Modern Opera Company.

My gratitude goes to the Vilcek Foundation, New York Foundation for the Arts, NYU Provost's Global Research Initiative fellowship, and NYU Shanghai for generous assistance and time that supported the making of these poems.

Thank you to Dana Prescott and the staff at Civitella Ranieri Foundation for deepenings and conjurings.

I remain indebted to my colleagues and students at NYU, Princeton University, and Bard College for the intellectual community and conversation.

Inestimable gratitude to Jeff Shotts for the editorial vision and innumerable generosities toward this work. And thanks to the team at Graywolf Press, for the steady commitment and care, visible on every page.

Thank you to Rigoberto González, Sally Wen Mao, and Cathy Park Hong for their deep kindness in taking time to read and offer words in support of this book.

Thank you to Albert, best of dogs, for myriad affections and playful distractions.

Thank you to the Shroffs and Joys for enduring forms of hospitality.

To my family—in New Jersey, Liverpool, Wuhu, and Hefei—without whom this book would not exist, and with whom there is nearness and witness: through you, all enlargements and continuations.

Thank you to Ravi, as ever, for all that language cannot reach.

JENNY XIE was born in Anhui, China, and resides in New York City. She is the author of a previous collection of poems, *Eye Level*, which was a finalist for the National Book Award and recipient of the Walt Whitman Award of the Academy of American Poets and the Holmes National Poetry Prize. Her chapbook, *Nowhere to Arrive*, received the Drinking Gourd Prize. She has taught at Princeton University and NYU, and is currently on faculty at Bard College.

The text of *The Rupture Tense* is set in Sabon MT Pro.
Book design by Rachel Holscher.
Composition by Bookmobile Design and Digital
Publisher Services, Minneapolis, Minnesota.
Manufactured by Versa Press on acid-free paper.